Barrow in Furness

A Photographic Recollection

compiled by Raymond Sankey

DALESMAN BOOKS
1974

The Dalesman Publishing Company Ltd., Clapham (via Lancaster), Yorkshire.
First Published 1974

ISBN: 0 85206 224 9

Cover illustrations: Front: Michaelson Road from the High Level Bridge. Back: Top: Shipyard workers stream across Walney Bridge. Bottom: Cavendish Street at the junction with Dalton Road.

Printed in Great Britain by
FRETWELL & BRIAN LTD.
Silsden, Nr. Keighley, Yorkshire.

Introduction
by J. Melville

HAVING HAD a strong interest in local history for many years, it was pleasing to be invited to write a short introduction to a series of photographs taken in Barrow-in-Furness in days gone by. On looking through the list I feel that there is scarcely one that could be taken to-day—the scenes have either entirely disappeared or else have radically changed. Some have been used as illustrations for newspaper articles, so I will restrict myself to outlining, very simply, a little of Barrow's history.

What is now Barrow-in-Furness was, 120 years ago, a collection of villages. Photographs of some of these, though partly modernised, are included and take our minds back to the days before Barrow began to develop. We are fortunate that some of those villages are still with us and these give interest and pleasure to both locals and visitors.

For more than 400 years Furness was ruled over by the Abbots of Furness Abbey, which was established in 1127 by a party of monks of the Order of Savigny who had been at Tulketh, near Preston, for four years previously. They changed over to the Cistercian Order in 1148. The site of their abbey, in the Vale of Nightshade, was chosen because there they would find seclusion as well as a ready supply of timber and stone for the buildings and an adequate source of water for domestic and sanitary purposes. The Cistercians were good agriculturalists and they gradually brought the land into a fair state of cultivation, establishing granges on the lines of what we would call "home farms". These have since developed into villages, many of which have been incorporated within the boundaries of Barrow-in-Furness. Numerous splendid photographs have been published showing the ruins of the abbey of St. Mary of Furness, so there has been no need to include any in this volume.

Barrow was originally "Barrai", which is Norse—"Bare Island"—and indicates the state of the immediate vicinity before the monks came. Furness is "Far Ness", the far point, thus describing the shape of the district as it would appear to newcomers after crossing the Kent and Leven estuaries from Lancaster. Hence we get Barrow-in-Furness.

Barrow began to assume a little importance due to the increased mining of iron ore around Lindal and Dalton. More ore was brought to the surface than could be used by the local furnaces at Backbarrow and Newland late in the 18th century, so the Backbarrow Company made an "Iron Floor" at Barrow in 1776 from which the ore was exported. This was followed by the Newland Iron Co. who built a quay at Barrow, used for the first time in 1782. With increased trade the company constructed a wooden jetty, about 100 yards long and projecting into the Barrow Channel, and from it they could load 100 tons a day. Trade from Barrow harbour now gradually increased. Three other jetties were built and Barrow became the principal place in Furness for the export of ore, although all the mineral had to be conveyed by horse and cart from mines to the jetties. Apart from the shipping trade, life went on as usual at the surrounding farms, with the occasional added interest during the summers of holiday visitors to Barrow and Rampside. Here they enjoyed sea bathing, which was then developing as a health-giving exercise.

In spite of the increased export trade, Barrow village in 1843 had less than 30 houses and some of those were only hovels. Unless much better transport facilities could be provided it was likely to grow very slowly. A number of schemes were investigated, but with little progress until Mr. H. W. Schneider began to be interested in the iron trade here. With the financial backing of the Dukes of Devonshire and Buccleuch and a few other influential gentlemen, the Furness Railway connecting the iron mines at Lindal and the slate quarries at Kirkby to Barrow and Rampside was opened in 1846. Barrow became its headquarters. This brought much better conditions to the harbour which, however, was still only a "Creek under the Port of Lancaster".

From that time progress accelerated. A young man, James Ramsden, had been appointed manager of the Engineering Department of the Furness Railway. He became secretary and general manager, and later a director, and under his energetic leadership—with the finance provided by the Dukes and others—expensive schemes were planned and carried out. One of the first was begun by Mr. Schneider and Robert Hannay in 1857, when they commenced the construction of the iron furnaces at Hindpool. These came into operation in 1859 and very quickly became a great success. In 1864 James

Ramsden launched a company to manufacture steel, and two years later an amalgamation of the iron works and the steel company formed the Barrow Haematite Iron and Steel Co. which soon had sixteen furnaces in operation.

Such a rapid surge in production drew personnel from other parts of the country and the resulting housing shortage caused grave concern. It was impossible to build houses quickly enough and, in an attempt to meet the situation, a Dundee Firm was engaged to erect a series of flats on the "Scotch Buildings Pattern". These served for about 90 years and, although they have been demolished in recent years, Mr. Sankey's photograph describes them better than any words of mine—even though my parents lived in one when they were first married.

The railway station was adjacent to the works in St. George's Square and the Strand, and the town developed from that area. The word "Strand" adequately described the principal road, for it ran alongside the Barrow Channel leading up to Hindpool. From the quay a large sea-borne trade, inwards and outwards, expanded to the extent that the Furness Railway directors decided to embark on the construction of the Devonshire and Buccleuch Docks, using the channel between the mainland and Barrow Island (Old Barrow, as it is still called) as the site. The first dock, the Devonshire, was opened on September 19th, 1867, in the presence of Mr. Gladstone by the Duke of Devonshire himself. Earlier in that year Barrow had obtained its Charter of Incorporation as a Borough and, after the opening of the dock, very optimistic speeches were delivered, one expression being that Barrow would rival Liverpool as a port—a prospect that appeared for a time to have some justification, but which subsequent events have proved to be a serious exaggeration.

Work was proceeding on Buccleuch Dock and plans for further extensive dock facilities were well in hand. The iron and steel works continued to prosper. A jute and flax works was put into operation in 1870, mainly to provide employment for the female population, and it became the largest jute factory in England. The corn mill was founded in 1871, while small shipbuilding firms had been established since 1847. Brickmaking and timber importing firms were also flourishing, but all these companies have now passed out of existence. However, another shipbuilding site, on which production began in 1872, has been greatly extended and is still one of the leaders in the country. It began as the Barrow Iron Shipbuilding Co. and has since borne the titles Barrow Shipbuilding Co.; Naval Construction and Armaments Co.; Vickers, Sons; Vickers, Sons and Maxim; Vickers Ltd.; Vickers Armstrongs; and now, again, Vickers Ltd. The works occupy a large proportion of the land on Barrow Island.

After Vickers, Sons and Co. took over in 1896 the firm became more and more involved in warship construction and, as the work expanded, more accommodation for workpeople became essential. The firm negotiated for the purchase of land on Walney Island where it proposed to build two estates of first class houses, Vickerstown North and Vickerstown South. While this work was in progress, 250 employees were accommodated for eighteen months in the cabins of an Atlantic liner, the "Alaska", which was moored in one of the docks.

Then, with the greatly increased population on Walney, the problem of transporting the workpeople to and from the island over Walney Channel again came up for serious consideration. Walney Ferry No. 1 had been put into service in 1878 after a great deal of agitation by residents, who repeatedly complained about the destruction of the old fords when the docks and harbour were made. It became inadequate after Vickerstown was built and a larger ferry, No. 2, was substituted in 1902. The improved service was never entirely satisfactory and pleas for a bridge across the channel, which had been put forward since 1887, continued with greater effort. Barrow Corporation and Vickers Ltd. were very much in favour of a bridge being constructed, but the Furness Railway directors were opposed on the grounds that it would interfere with navigation. It was only after prolonged discussions that plans for the bridge were approved. It was opened on July 30th, 1908, although everyone using it had to pay a toll.

Photographs of the bridge under construction and its opening are included in this series, while there is also one taken later showing it being freed from tolls by the Duke and Duchess of York on April 4th, 1935. Other photographs show one of the ferries and also scenes on Walney Island—Biggar village; Biggar Bank (a large public recreation area); and James Dunn Park which had been provided by Vickers. These indicate some of the open-air facilities for both townsfolk and visitors alike.

A little more must be said of the development of the town itself. The census return of 1851 lists a total population of 501 in Barrow, Barrow Island and Hindpool, but by 1874 the population of the Borough had risen to 35,000 and by 1911 to nearly 64,000. At one period during the 1914/18 war it reached more than 75,000 but now it is back to about 64,000. A number of the photographs show parts of the town during what was, perhaps, the time of its greatest prosperity. Scenes illustrate some of the shops; the dress of both male and female inhabitants; different types of public transport, from steam-driven trams to electric traction; crowds of workmen making their way to the shipbuilding and engineering works; women war workers in 1914/18. All of them give a glimpse of the general atmosphere of the town more than fifty years ago. Readers looking at some of these pictures cannot fail to be impressed with the wide, tree-lined main roads which our forefathers planned, somewhat ahead of their time, but for which we are now truly thankful in view of modern traffic conditions.

Moving further out of the town centre, which has now been almost entirely rebuilt, we are taken to some of the suburbs built during the first decade of this century. As the main centre moved from the Strand, the Furness Railway constructed a new loop line from Salthouse to Ormsgill and erected a new Central station adjacent to Abbey Road. This is illustrated, and the picture forms a useful record of a Victorian structure which is no longer with us as it was demolished by enemy action in 1941 and has since been rebuilt on more modern lines.

More outlying places within the Borough have not been neglected. Besides Rampside, there is a photograph of Roa Island to which the railway company constructed an embankment and ran through trains from main line stations. From the pier on the island steamer services sailed to Ireland, the Isle of Man, Blackpool, Fleetwood and Liverpool before Ramsden Dock was completed. In another direction is Hawcoat, while just below that village is High Cocken where there still remains a cottage in which George Romney, the celebrated painter, lived during his early life. These are only a few of the semi-rural scenes which still remain within the Borough.

Very few illustrations of industry in the town are included in this series, but attention is drawn to that of the launch of the "Orama", built for the Orient Steam Navigation Co. by Vickers Ltd. and completed in the works in 1924. It was the forerunner of a whole series of large passenger liners constructed in the works during succeeding years.

Mention has been made of the Duke and Duchess of York, who visited the town in 1935. Barrow has been favoured with a number of Royal visitors during this century, and another illustration shows the Prince of Wales (later Edward VIII), during his visit in 1927 when he opened Infield Mansion. This was given by Vickers as a convalescent home for the people of Barrow, but unfortunately it has now been demolished.

It is confidently hoped that this series of photographs of Barrow taken between the years 1900 and 1935 will prove of interest, not only to Barrovians, but also to many others who have a desire to know what Barrow-in-Furness was like during those years. They are full of local history.

Biggar village, Walney Island.

The Queen's Arms at Biggar.

The swings on Biggar Bank.

Remains of old windmill at Walney, finally demolished in the 1939-45 war.

Above: James Dunn Park, Walney; the upper view of about 1906 shows a pierrot concert in progress.

Opposite: Bank Holiday crowds on Biggar Bank about 1907 (top and centre), and on Walney Beach.

James Dunn Park, the Ferry Hotel and the steam ferry which until 1908 connected the island with Barrow.

A close-up of the steam ferry, packed to capacity with men and animals.

Building Walney Bridge, which replaced the ferry.

A sailing ship passing through Walney Bridge.

The official opening of the bridge on July 30th, 1908.

The Barrow-Fleetwood steamer "Philomel" taking part in the Walney Bridge opening ceremonies.

Walney Bridge from James Dunn Park. Central Drive now passes through the point where the photograph was taken.

Above: Ocean Road (top) before the advent of the Biggar Bank tram service, shown in the bottom picture on the formal opening day.

Opposite: Naval Airship No. 1 (top), better known as "Mayfly", was built at Barrow in 1911. Its nickname was a misnomer, for it suffered a disaster and never did fly (centre). The bottom picture shows Airship R80, built in 1921, flying over Duke Street.

R.80

PUBLIC S
NG BATH

Above: Shipyard employees head for work along Michaelson Road and across the High Level Bridge (top). Barrow Corn Mill (bottom).

Opposite: Buccleuch Dock Bridge, dismantled about 1971 (top). High Level Bridge (centre). Barrow Public Swimming Bath proved a non-swimmer in a gale, and foundered in Cavendish Dock (bottom).

Michaelson Road in the days when trams ran down its centre. The building on the left corner was a bakehouse, then a cinema and is now a canteen.

Michaelson Road from the town end, showing on the left what was then the main post office.

Duke Street about 1910. Sandwiched between the Majestic Hotel and the Town Hall is the fire station.

Scotch Buildings at Hindpool which were badly damaged by bombs in 1941 and have since been demolished. In the centre of the picture is the ash pit.

Rush hour at Cavendish Square.

In a quieter moment a bicycle is about to cross the tram lines.

The Strand, showing buildings which have now almost entirely been demolished. The notice board on the right carries the coat-of-arms of King Edward VII and the words "Recruiting Office: Royal Navy and Royal Marines."

The Higher Grade School, with a tramcar approaching.

Above: Shoppers casually stroll down the middle of Dalton Road in the days before the motor car. A policeman has little to do except chat to passers-by.

Opposite: Two views of Ship Street. In the upper photograph coal and other necessities are being delivered, while children congregate between the Devonshire Hotel and the shop of a Mr. Honeyman who was both a butcher and a fruiterer. The lower view shows washing day in full force, with a variety of commodious garments strung between the tall tenements.

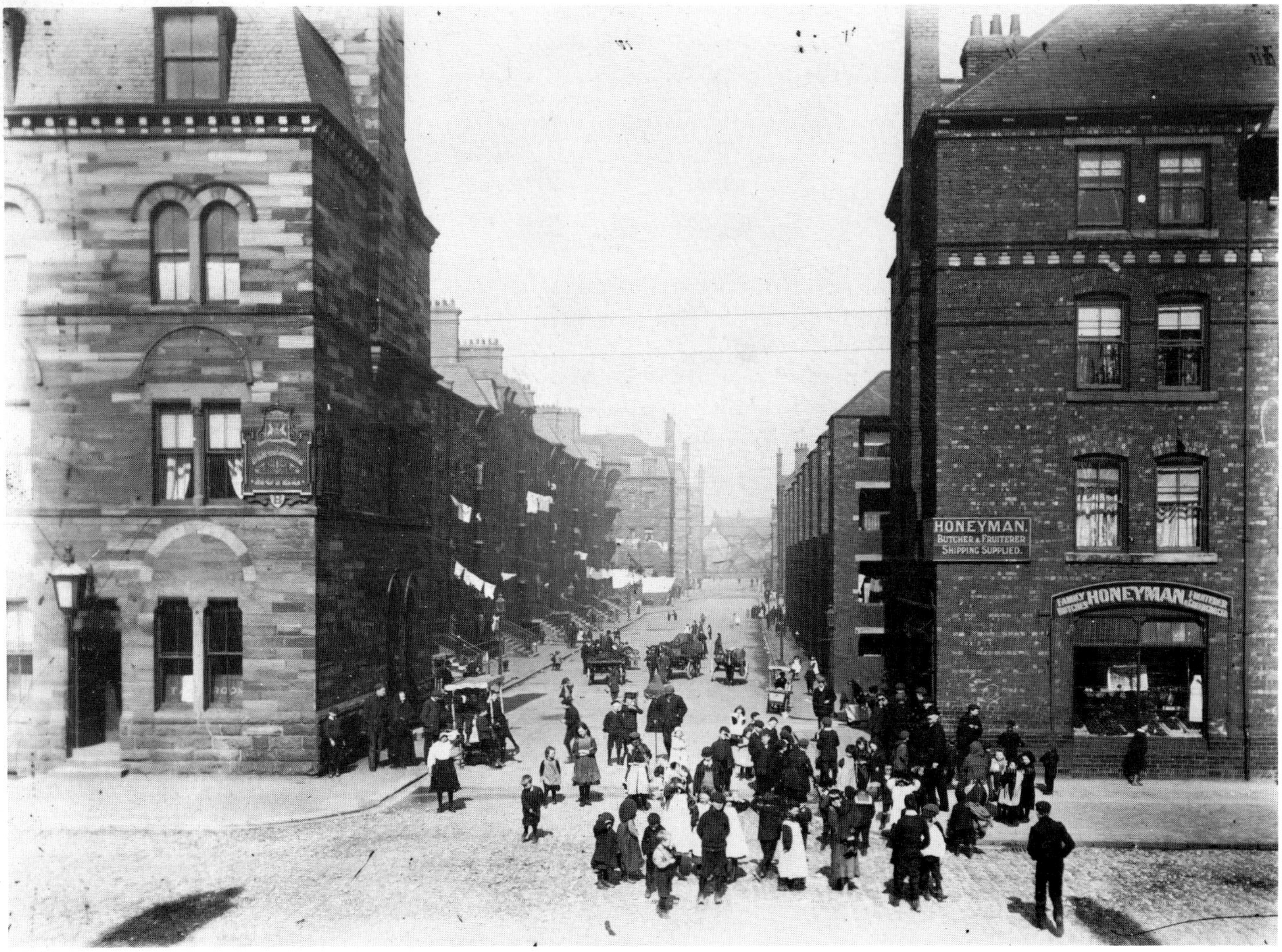
HONEYMAN.
BUTCHER & FRUITERER
SHIPPING SUPPLIED.
HONEYMAN

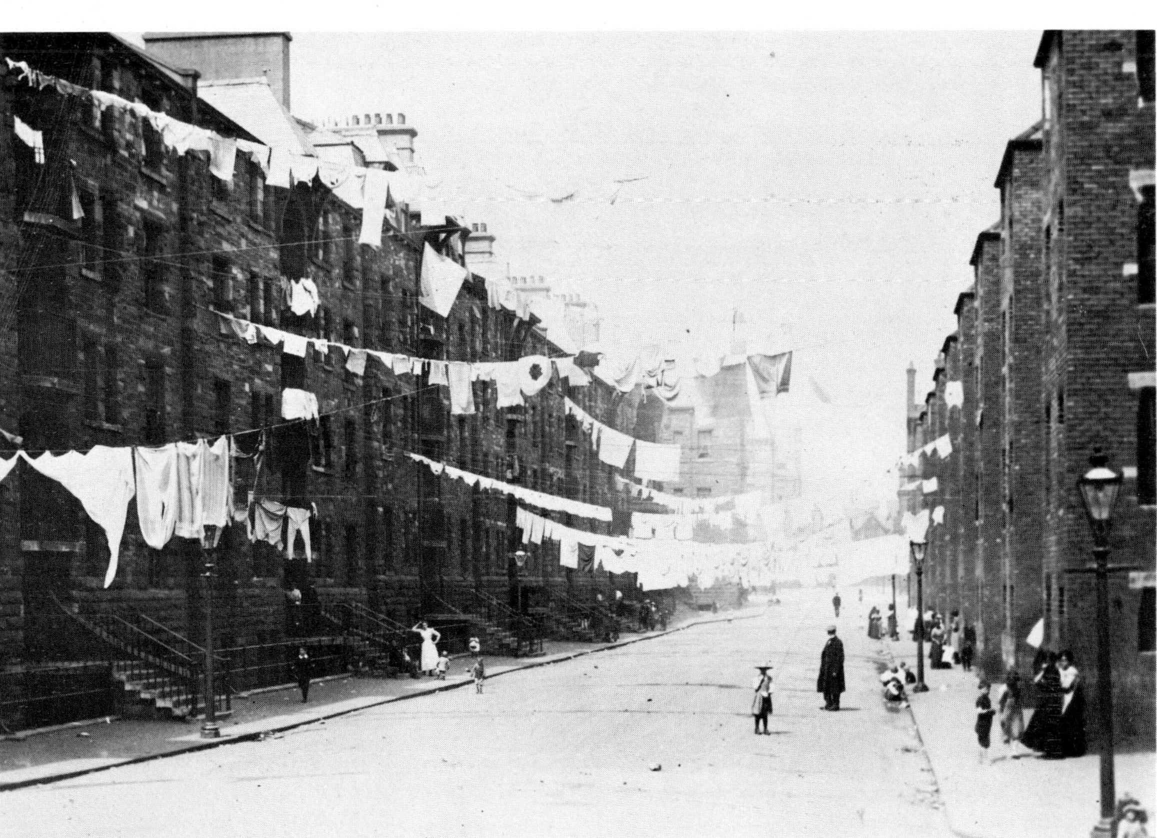

Cavendish Street from Duke Street. The value of street advertising was already recognised.

Cavendish Street in 1913. Note the figure of a Scotsman above the tobacconists' shop on the extreme right.

A motley crowd at the entrance to Paxton Street, which has now been completely demolished to make way for the new town centre.

The Bull Hotel at the corner of Paxton Street and Dalton Road was very well known in the old days.

Duke Street, with the County Auction Rooms on the left.

Station Hill, Abbey Road. On the right is "The Stadium", burnt down in 1914.

Barrow Central station, opened in 1882 and destroyed by bombs in 1941. It has since been replaced by a structure in modern styling.

The exterior of the station, showing on the right the glass cage which housed "Coppernob", one of the original Furness Railway locomotives of 1846.

Furness Abbey station, situated in sylvan surroundings.

Piel station on Roa Island, until 1882 the embarkation point for steamers to the Isle of Man and Belfast.

Barrow Shipyard station.

Rampside station on the branch to Piel.

A tramcar passes the "White House", Abbey Road.

The tram halt at the Town Hall. The double-deck tramcars on the left were used on the Abbey and Walney routes, but were too tall for the Salthouse Bridge route which was served by single-deck cars of the type seen on the right.

One of the early steam trams at the Abbey terminus in Abbey Road.

A single-deck tramcar in Abbey Road near Croslands Park.

The tram passing loop in Abbey Road near the corner of Dalton Road and Hartington Street. An early motor car is being pursued by a double-deck tram. On the left is the Gaiety Picture House and the Salvation Army Hall.

A tramcar in Abbey Road. Diverging on the left is Hawcoat Lane with a drinking fountain in the centre of the road.

Girls and boys come out to play at Hawcoat village.

Romney's early home, left on the edge of a precipice by quarrying operations.

Above: Hawcoat Lane (top). Strawberry Lane (now Hollow Lane) from Abbey Road (bottom).

Opposite: Newbarns village and the Farmers' Arms before and after the widening of the road (top and centre). Furness Abbey Hotel, built by the Furness Railway and demolished after being damaged by bombs in 1941 (bottom).

An early Daimler motor bus in Duke Street.

A similar vehicle outside the Old Market Hall.

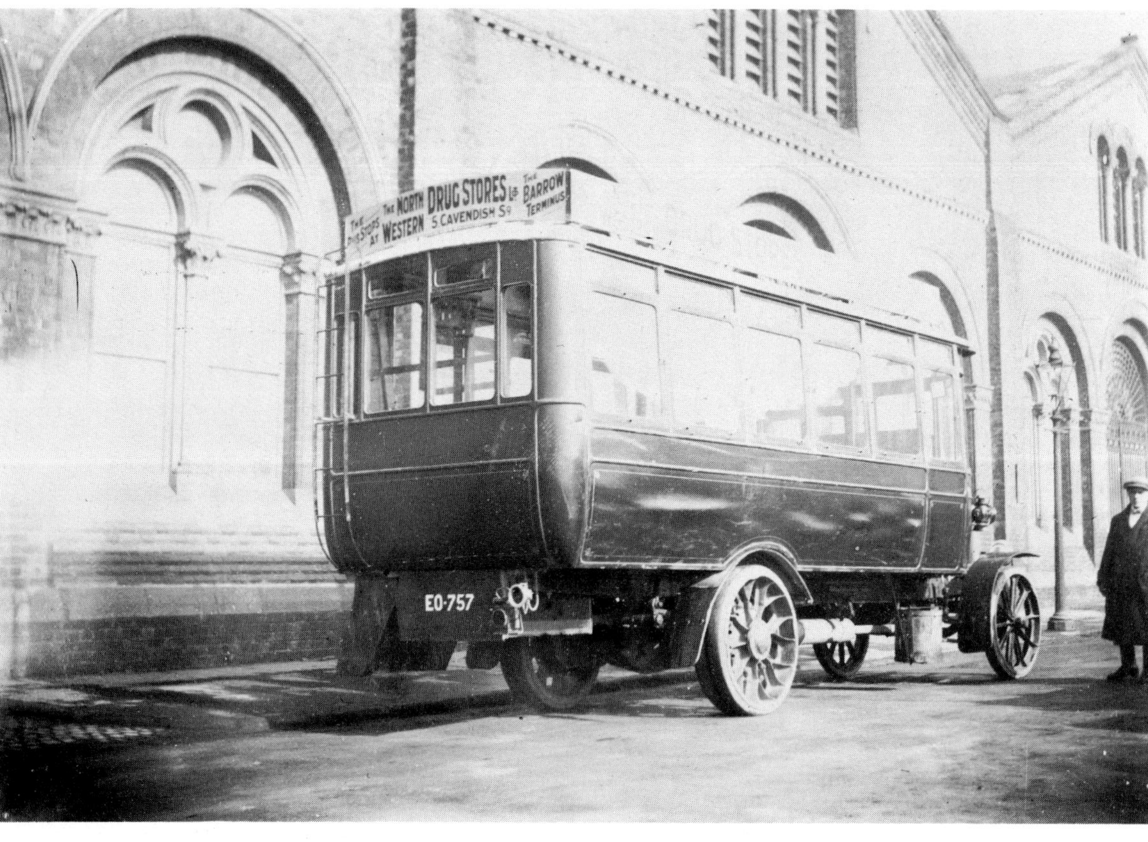

A 1912 view of the Barrow Fire Station in Duke Street, on the site now occupied by the Magistrates' Court. As the poster shows, it was about to be replaced by a new fire station in Abbey Road.

The one-time pride and joy of the fire brigade. "Catherine Butler", a Merryweather fire engine with a Hatfield pump.

King George V visits Vickers Works in 1915.

The Prince of Wales opens Infield Home.

The Duchess of York (the present Queen Mother) renames Walney Bridge as Jubilee Bridge and frees it of its former toll.

The Duke and Duchess of York on board H.M.S. Ajax during their 1935 visit to Barrow. This ship later won fame at the Battle of the River Plate.

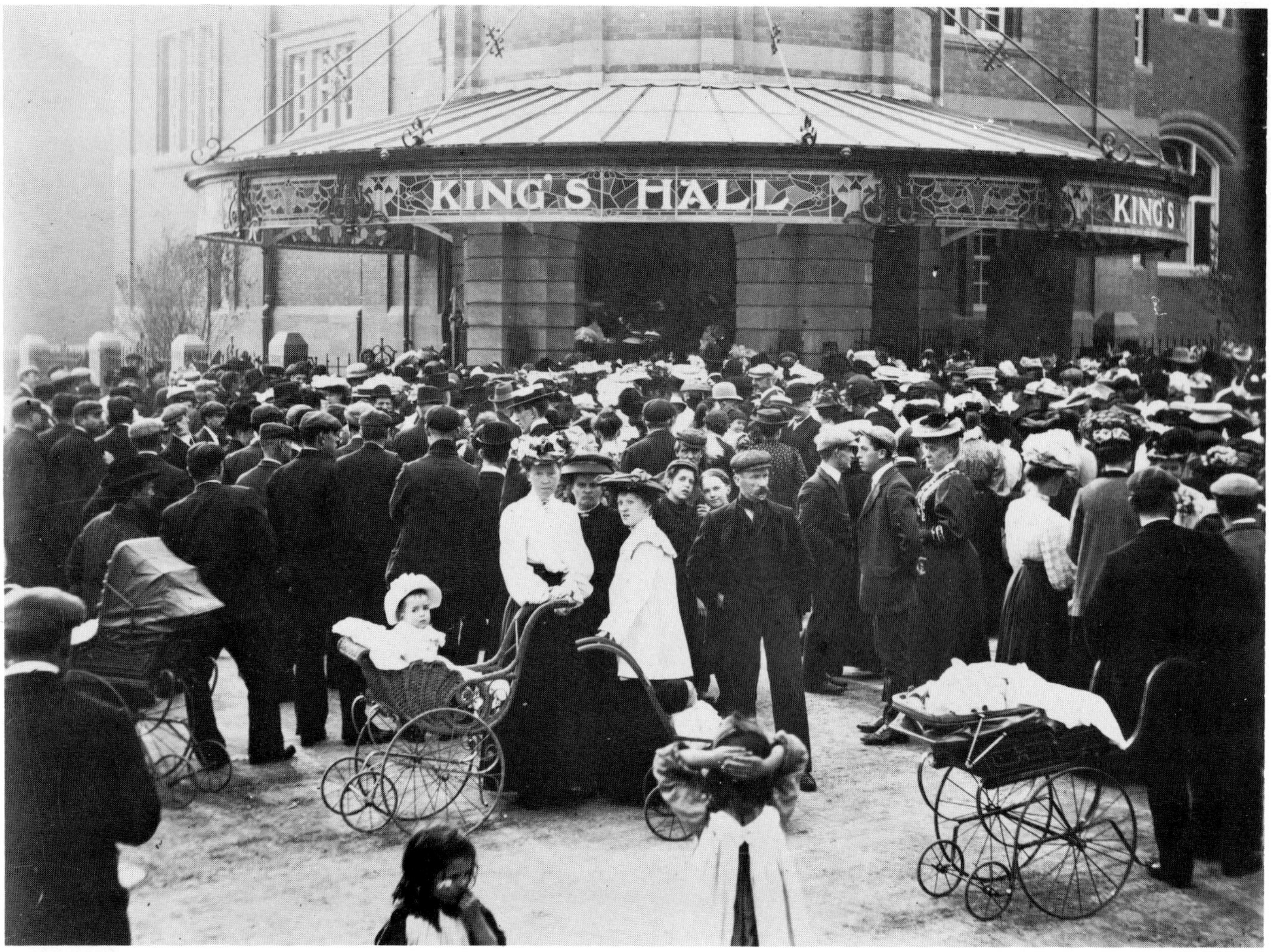
KING'S HALL
KING'S

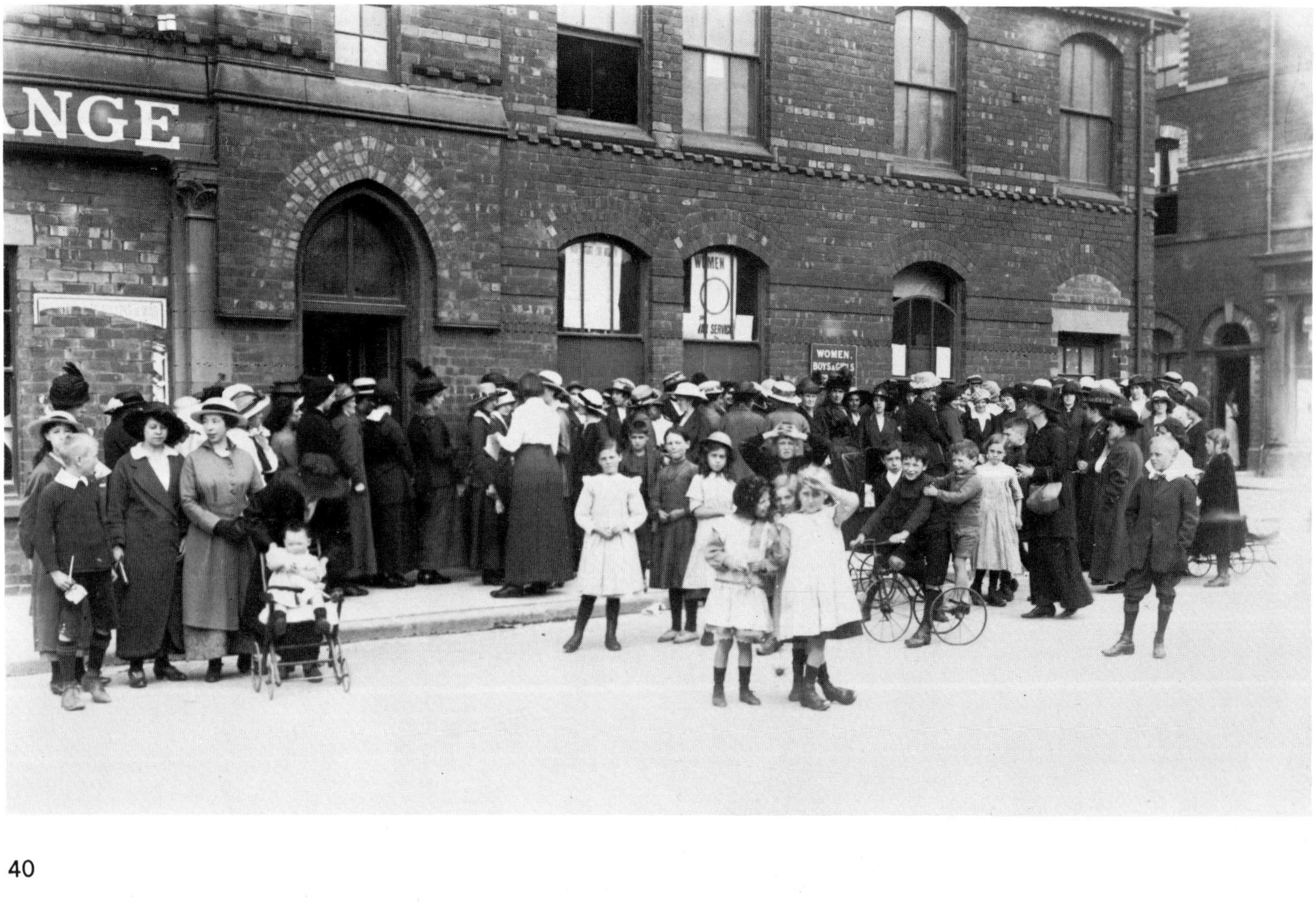
NGE
WOMEN
WOMEN, BOYS & GIRLS

Above: Raising the flag at the start of building the Salvation Army Hall in Abbey Road.

Opposite: The opening of King's Hall (top). Enrolment of women war workers in the 1914-18 war.

Pierrot show in the Park, 1908.

Progress comes to Vickerstown houses in the form of the first delivery of electric cookers (below). Barrow Corporation Electricity Department's stand at an exhibition in the Drill Hall (opposite).

BARROW CORPORATION ELECTRICITY SUPPLY.
ELECTRIC MOTORS
SUPERIOR & LESS COST
THAN ANY OTHER POWER
MAY BE HAD ON HIRE
LOW RATES
CALORITE
ELECTRIC IRONS
WONDERFUL! 20 HOURS FOR ONE PENNY!

"Lady Moyra", the best-known of the Furness Railway's Barrow-Fleetwood steamers, which made her last Morecambe Bay trip in September 1914. She sailed on the Bristol Channel after 1919 and was sunk at Dunkirk.

The launch of "Orama", the first of a series of ships built for the Orient Line and one which marked the end of the depression years.